Top 16 covert emotional manipulation tactics

12 Ways to Take Control in Personal Relationships

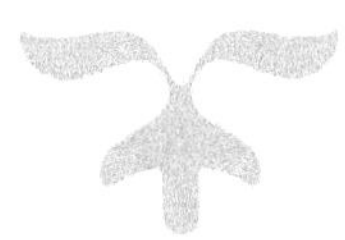

by David Newman

Hidden emotional manipulation in a modern society occurs quite often and represents a serious problem in building relationships between people in different spheres of life. You may discover by chance that you are manipulated by someone you know – that may be your workmate, boy- or girlfriend, one of your relatives or just anyone you deal with in interpersonal relationships.

In most cases, people with low self-esteem are at the highest risk of becoming victims of manipulation: they, step by step, are getting involved in the relationships, where they are the object of the manipulative influence of another person.

Psychologists state that people with psychological disorders are prone to manipulation, which, in fact, induce them to such behavior. Psychological manipulation harms not only the feelings of the victims but also the manipulators themselves because finally, they turn to be self-isolated in their attempts to dominate and control other people and relationships overall.

Although nowadays, due to interest in psychology, many people have learned to make out the manipulative influence of others, often psychological manipulations take new forms, so it becomes increasingly difficult to identify them. The question that now arises in front of many people is how to determine if they are victims of manipulation, and if so, how to cope with it, maintaining psychological stability and not harming relations with significant others.

The experts in psychology have identified certain traits common to all manipulators, and here are some of them:

- they tend to move towards achieving their goals by using other people;
- they crave for power and feel the need to have superiority in the relationship;
- have a low self-esteem and strive to have domination over others to increase their perception of own importance;

If you found the above behavioral traits from someone you know, be aware of their actions and care of yourself so as not to become an object of manipulative influence.

But if you want to learn not only to spot manipulators and their tactics, be able to defend yourselves from them, read our book.

Here you will read:

- how to understand if you are manipulated;
- what manipulative tactics are used by manipulators to gain what they want and how you can identify them;
- what types manipulators exist over there;
- how you can defend yourself from psychological manipulations.

We wish you a pleasant reading.

Table of Contents

Chapter 1. Manipulation in daily life: how do people become victims of manipulation and who are the manipulators?

The techniques of hidden emotional manipulation are insidious methods of control that some people use against others, pursuing their personal goals. The methods of manipulation are misleading tactics that are aimed at changing your behavior and perception, herewith hidden manipulation works beyond your conscious understanding. Victims generally have no idea that they are being manipulated when this occurs, that's why it is so important to be aware of the methods that the manipulator applies to you. You should remember the rule that you will play the role of a puppet in someone's scenario as long as you do not realize how easy your consciousness may come under manipulation by other people.

So who are these people who manipulate others?

The most skillful and toxic manipulators are those people whose inalienable features of character are psychopathy, narcissism, Machiavellianism. Those are individuals who have no empathy, so they manipulate others according to own plan and reasons and do not care what it costs for the person being manipulated. These individuals use others to achieve their own goals with attempts to hide this fact. Such people manipulate others deliberately so that to carry out own ambitions or gain their ends.

Manipulative individuals try to hide who they are in fact, creating a winsome, pleasant and positive image, so at first glance, it seems that they really are such as they claim to be. But despite their feigned benevolence, they continue to keep their malicious intent, in the further implementation of which they ultimately harm the mental health of people who are in close contact with them.

On the other hand, there are a lot of individuals, who use manipulation unconsciously, not realizing, what they are doing. People without serious psychological issues also resort to manipulation to get from others what they want, without bad intent, and often without realizing what they are doing. You may spot manipulative traits in the behavior of your friend, neighbor, one of your relatives, workmate or boss. From time to time we manipulate others rather than directly tell them about the things which we would like them to do for us or something else, that we want to get from them. At this rate, we are all to blame for manipulative actions and inclinations.

Nevertheless, it is necessary to make a clear demarcation line between those, who is the pathological manipulator, and the people, who apply the manipulations on occasions. Pathological manipulators have no other ways of interacting with others except manipulative actions and influences, as well as they cannot experience deep feelings and bestow to their partner's anything like love, care, devotion and so one that is common for healthy romantic relationships. And there are no means that you can make them change their behavior.

The result of someone's manipulative actions is the fact that your ability to consciously make decisions gradually is being undermined, and thus you even do not realize, how you lose your tendency to act on your own interests, in alignment with your values, goals, and principles. In other words, under the influence of manipulation, you are inclined to actions that you would not have done in other circumstances.

Another dark side of manipulation is that it diminishes your self-confidence and self-esteem. You can force yourself to compromise with yourself right up to losing self-esteem and developing a distorted concept of reality, and thus you may get rid of your belief in own feeling of reality and perception. Because of the low level of self-defense, you actually become vulnerable to any manipulative impacts in the future.

And one day it may turn out that your self-esteem and emotional well-being have been given to the power of manipulator, and you find that your imagination and judgments about yourself, as well as your self-value, depend on the opinion of the manipulator. As soon as this manipulative person discovers that you are on her or his hook, they will destroy your identity step by step. So you are at high risk of radically changing your personality for worse or complete destruction of it. And undoubtedly, the consequences for your psychological health will be deplorable.

To achieve success in the implementation of their manipulative tactics, the manipulator, first of all, tend to study your character, habits, behavior - and all this is not just because he is interested in your personality in itself. This person will study your personality to identify vulnerabilities in your character, hereafter he/she will be able to use this knowledge of you to turn you into their puppet that would do all they desire.

Do not expect that they will regret their actions, even if they have caused you a lot of pain and suffering. They are ruthless enough not to take care about negative effects for others caused by their manipulations. All that matters for them is to set their control over somebody and get from this person what they are striving towards.

If you become more aware of the main manipulative tactics, that people use to turn others into their puppets, you will be able to recognize someone's covert attempts of to psychologically subjugate you to their will and therefore defend yourself from latent aggression. But it is not always easy to do since the manipulators tend to rely on your trust, doubts and strong emotions, including feelings of love, guilt, fear, so as to prevent you from sound thinking and ability to recognize their manipulation. In many cases, they deliberately provoke you to emotions for this purpose, and in such a way manage to get away with the disclosure of their manipulations and punishment for it. Therefore, when you doubt own perception or have an emotion that makes you exposed to manipulation, it is very important to realize it, take control of your emotions and pull yourself together.

Chapter 2. Caution, Manipulation! How to determine if you are the victim of manipulations

This chapter describes the ways how you can determine if you are being manipulated or are in manipulative relationships.

The manipulation methods that people may seem to be different, but if you take a closer look, many of them are similar to each other.

If you are a victim of manipulation, it may arise a vague feeling that something is wrong, but you cannot define exactly what.

Does someone use manipulations against you? Of cause, you may suspect that you are being manipulated, but you also may have some doubts if it is really so. Also, you may suppose that all those admissions concerning the manipulative impact of another person are only your attempts to explain to yourself that strange feeling of psychological discomfort that has arisen recently during your communicating with a certain person. Whatever it might be, you want to get certain answers to your uncertain questions. And how can you determine that this is so?

In fact, it's easier and more obvious than you might think. The most reasonable in this case is to study the technique, which manipulator use in their relationships with other people to get what they want. You may also explore the key psychological features of manipulative personalities so that be more skillful in your knowledge of people's behavior and your ability to spot manipulators as such in general. But the truth is that it is not necessary to learn anything to figure out if you are been manipulated. The simplest and most effective way to understand if you are being manipulated is to observe yourself, your feelings, behavior, and emotional reactions and try to understand yourself, and what is wrong particularly with you. First of all, you must answer the following questions for yourself:

- What has changed in my feeling, behavior, and emotional reactions recently?

- What do I feel while communicating with that particular person?

- Do I really want to carry out those actions that I do under his influence?

- Do I feel happy or depressed the last time?

- What about my self-confidence? Is it OK?

- Does my feeling of self-worth depend on that particular person?

- Do I sacrifice my own goals, values and principles in order to make that particular person feel happier, more kind to me etc.?

In search of answers to the above questions, you will be able to analyze in detail and understand not only yourself but also the essence of your relationship with another person. Your findings in the field of introspection and analysis of relationships may surprise you, but not always they may have a positive connotation. But whatever conclusions you might draw, you should remember that you are a full-fledged person, and your life belongs only to you, therefore you should not, in any case, let someone dispose of you, your feelings and your life for the sake of achieving their own goals.

So, as a result of analyzing your actions and relationships with another person, you began to assume that you are the object of manipulative influence, although you can not state this with complete certainty. What should be considered and what to pay attention to in this situation? If you have figured out that you are being manipulated, you must remember, that manipulation is harmful not only for our mindset but also our personality and psychological health on the whole, even if do not realize that it is taking place in our life.

Below we point out some key signs that can indicate the fact that you are exposed to manipulation by another person. So, you can be sure that your boyfriend or girlfriend manipulates you in such cases:

- You are unhappy in a relationship, and you feel uncertain about it most of the time, but still remain in awe of losing it, because you are unbelievably happy in it from time to time;

- You feel angry or upset with someone;

- You are eager to make your partner happy; you are trying your best, but are not sure that you have reached a breakthrough in your endeavors. You feel that you really do not know what can bring joy to your partner, and how you can make him happy. You are trying hard, but it seems that there are no long-term results.

- You do things that do not suit you, which are contrary to your nature, which contradict your values, limitations, and do not match your capabilities, to make your partner happy or not to damage your relationship.

- You often get the feeling that you are at risk of destroying the best relationships that have ever existed in your life, but you do not know what exactly you are doing wrong, and which exactly actions are shattering your relationship;

- Your mood depends entirely on the relationship, which causes that you may feel extremely fine or bad in regard to your relationship;

- Your feeling of being happy from getting love gradually fades and turns into fear that you can lose this love;

- You feel that there is no clarity in the relationship; they seem to be a complex puzzle. You often feel that there is a lack of certainty in your relationship, and it is difficult for you to explain to yourself and others the essence and nature of these relationships;

- You involuntarily notice that your relationship turns into a kind of obsession for you: you carefully analyze every word spoken by you or your partner, each your and his or her action, every event in your relationship. Moreover, you constantly discuss all this with people who are not involved in your relationship. But as a rule, the result of all this is by no means positive;

- You are often tormented by the feeling that something is really wrong, but what exactly, you are not able to identify;

- In many cases, your partner has indicated to you that you gave rise to a problem of mutual credence, jealousy, exaggerated reaction and anger;

- You do not have a clear certainty where, in what and how to support your partner, and this causes a feeling of insecurity, confusion, anxiety, and fear for your relationship;

- You feel that you are prohibited from expressing negative emotions and thoughts; therefore you restrain yourself in this, keeping these feelings to yourself. You feel frustrated because of the inability to talk about things that concern you.

- Your attitude to yourself, own dignity and your sense of joy of life have been greatly affected since the moment you started a relationship with a particular person.

- You got a feeling of less confidence, less intelligence, less sensibility and trust, less attractiveness, less security, or much more "less" in something positive than it was before relationships;

- You often feel guilty about something, and you find that you are apologizing a lot. You always try to correct mistakes, the reason for which, as you believe, you are. You blame yourself for the fact that your partner is pulling away from you. You can not explain how and why you tend to ruin your relationship;

- Every time you follow your sayings and actions to be better in the eyes of your significant other, to deserve him or her approval and get their favor again;

- Although you have never before been prone to erupting anger and other negative emotions, periodically you have explosions of anger, during which you burst into a rage and emotions of disappointment. In such cases, you to promise that this will not happen again, but no matter how you tried, it still happens again and again;

- You always feel that your actions do not satisfy the desires of your partner. He often indicates to you that you are always doing something wrong, as he wants, or says that you do everything wrong. You understand that in principle, you can never do everything "right", as your partner would have wished. Sometimes you get the idea that it is impossible for you to achieve the level of expectations that your partner has established;

- You often find yourself trying to learn more about your partner through the Internet: you are looking for information about him in social networks, aspire to check through the Internet search history what he is interested in, you can not calm down because you want to know the content of his email messages and his or her texts in messengers. You sometimes use geolocation function to find out where he or she is at the moment when he or she is not somewhere nearby.

So, if you find at least some of the listed points in your relationship, you have every reason to conclude that you are in a manipulative relationship.

But it is worth making one reservation on this issue, and it is this: if all your relationships are manipulative and you suffer from the fact that you tend to have to take upon yourself the role of a victim in each case, then maybe you have a certain psychological problem, or psychological complexes over which you can work on together with a specialist in psychology - whether it is a psychological consultant, a psychoanalyst, or even a psychotherapist.

1. The main types of manipulators we may face in daily life

In this chapter, we will focus on who are those individuals, whom we call manipulators, what traits distinguish them from others, what features are inherent in their behavior, and most importantly, how to learn to identify the manipulator among the people you know and deal with.

Manipulators use tactics that mislead another person to achieve what they want, with disastrous consequences for that person. Therefore, we can certainly argue that manipulation is a form of deception, and is characterized by the fact that people behave dishonestly in their actions and feelings.

Below, we described the main features of the behavior and character of a person, which indicate that he is a typical manipulator. We also tried to describe the basic manipulative tactics that some people use against others to use them in achieving their goals. While interacting with a particular person, you may notice that one of the manipulative techniques is used, either few of them or all at the same time.

Before we list the typical methods of manipulation, we recall that the manipulative individual will first carefully study the nature of his victim, afterward he or she chooses the most suitable mean to apply in the implementation of the plan regarding particular person chosen as an object of their manipulation.

So, to indirectly achieve their goals by manipulating a particular person, the manipulative individual uses the following techniques.

2. The tactics of positive support

In order to force you to fulfill his or her desires, the person manipulating you will use positive support. This means this individual tends to:

- express superficial sympathy when you are sad, or when something bad happens to you or in your life;

- use feigned allure;

- apologize more than necessary;

- bestow you money, gifts, endorsement to get what they want;

- use a fake smile or laughter to trigger a positive reaction.

All this manipulator can use to win your trust and favorable attitude to him or her, giving you some kind of bait in the form of positive feelings, emotions, nevertheless not gratis, but in order to subsequently get from you what they want.

3. Negative support

The tactic of using negative support is that you get rid of negative situations, provided that you fulfill the requirements of your significant other. He can tell you that you will not have to do the things that you do not like doing, if you fulfill his request, or do what he demands of you. Thus, the manipulator provides you with a reward or getting rid of the negative situation in order to achieve their goal. Nevertheless, before realizing the fact of manipulation and giving the manipulator what he wants, the object of manipulation, in the end, may figure out that, having rid of one problem he or she faces another one, and such a situation may last infinitely long.

4. Mixed support

With this type of manipulation, only sometimes you receive from your significant other approval, praise, or what he or promises you in return for what he demands from you. This is reminiscent of the carrot and stick method: sometimes the manipulator gives you some positive reinforcement, but at some other time it happens on the contrary - when in response to your actions you get a negative reaction from that person.

But often this positive support for many people is so important that they always do something that the manipulator likes or demands of his victim. And in spite of the fact that the victim of manipulation might understand that positive support will not always occur, he or she will try hard for the sake of another person all the time.

Nevertheless, it will hardly come to the mind of the victim that this kind of relationship is of manipulative nature, and do not go to your advantage and in most cases, they cause your physical fatigue, emotional exhaustion, frustration and feeling that you are not appreciated enough.

5. Tactics of punishment

People who try to force you to do what they want by means of manipulative tricks will use punishment if they feel that the above methods cannot influence you. Thus, they use a stick to get your obedience to their goals and requirements. This negative treatment may include the following:

- Gloominess;

- Play in silence;

- Grumble;

- Intimidation;

- Emotional blackmail;

- Howls;

- Threats;

- Swearing;

- Crying;

- Playing the victim;

- Use of guilt.

The manipulator knows that this type of emotional blackmail will subdue the victim to their power. All this plays upon the heartstrings of the object of manipulation, badly impacting his or her psychological well-being, thus forcing this person to give in to the manipulator without realizing the harm he or she inflicts himself or herself by conceding to the manipulator.

6. Deceitfulness

One way to minimize the risk of being deceived is to understand that there are people who, because of psychopathic inclinations, lie all the time. When you catch them in lies, they will do everything to prove that you are mistaking in your assumptions about their lies. They will justify themselves, seek excuses, falsify facts, use inaccurate information - all that is necessary to keep you on the hook.

It is difficult to catch someone on a lie, but if you succeeded, do not forget about it and do not hide it. A lie in a relationship is very dangerous and indicates that something is wrong.

In spite of the fact that you can immediately lose confidence in the person whom you have caught in a lie, he or she will do everything possible to keep his influence on you. They will try to make you believe that their lies are not as terrible as you think, or try to prove that it was just some kind of misunderstanding. On the other hand, the manipulator can actually pretend that their victim is to blame for their lies. Playing on the guilt, the manipulator will be easier to achieve from the victim of their goals, and at the same time remain attached to the person who is the object of their negative influence.

In addition to all this, remember that being silent is also a kind of a lie, and you should not underestimate its strength. The lie by silence is to conceal the necessary information in order to provoke different reactions. Thus, the manipulator can use the concealment of information to keep the victim in a position where he or she can not make informed decisions.

7. Negation of guilt

To establish control over the victim is one of the goals that the manipulator sets. Periodically he can weaken or strengthen this control, but one thing is certain: the victim must always be subordinate to the manipulator and be under his full influence. Therefore, it is so important for the manipulative individual that the object of his manipulations never question his words and actions, otherwise, it creates for the manipulator the threat that his victim may get out of his control, and therefore the relationship as a whole between the manipulator and his victim may suffer. Therefore, there will never be a case in which the manipulator recognizes his mistakes, misses, or guilt. If something goes wrong, such an individual will always blame anyone rather himself. Thereby, when they are to blame for something, they will always use the negation of their guilt in combination with a lie.

And often this lie will concern the actions of other people. That is why this tactic may also be called a game in the search for the guilty.

8. Appealing to rationality

When we talk about manipulation, under appealing to rationality, or, rationalization, we mean the situations where the manipulator in the attempts to find an excuse for his or her improper actions or incorrect behavior, appeals to common sense or rationality. Thus, based on rationality, manipulators can explain their actions in almost any situation.

If to talk about rationalization, particularly in a situation where both the manipulator and the victim are involved, the manipulator, as a rule, blames his or her victim. In this case, in that this individual did this way, and committed incorrect actions, the guilty, according to him, is his victim. In this case, the denial of the own guilt combined with rationalization can serve as another tool for psychological influence on the victim. All the actions of the manipulator in these relationships are aimed at retaining power over the victim and controlling his or her actions, in order to use this person in achieving their own goals.

9. Diminishment

When you are upset with the manipulator or feel that his words or actions offend you, he or she will try to reduce everything to a joke, as if what he said or did is not as important or serious as you perceive that. But in fact, the manipulative individual sought to hurt you or the person he or she manipulated.

Reduction tactics are designed to take the feelings of the victim to the background, make the one feel secondary, insignificant as if he or she plays a supporting role in the relationship with the manipulator. Thus, the person is being manipulated, as a result of the tactic of understatement used by the manipulator starts believing that his feelings and emotions are less important. This behavior of the manipulator strikes a blow to the self-worth of the victim, therefore, the person who is manipulated may have a feeling that nobody consider his or her feelings if they are people of the "second class". In this way, the manipulator enhances the psychological impact on the victim, increasing the one's vulnerability to further manipulative actions.

10.   Distracting maneuvers and excuses

Every time you try to get a clear answer to a direct question, the manipulator will try to get off the answer in many ways. To get away from the answer, the manipulative individual will either answer vaguely or try to drop a topic and shunt the conversation on another subject of interest.

In this case, the ultimate intention of the manipulator is to confuse the interlocutor, forcing his or her to doubt the real version of events. Thus, the manipulator is able to use the victim's confusion in own interests.

Over time, the victim can really get confused by the information that the manipulator provides, and ultimately it may be difficult for him or her to distinguish between information that relates to real facts and messages that have nothing to do with reality and are just fiction, a lie, invented by the manipulator, to mislead and bewilder his victim. Thus, the object of the manipulation can find out that as a result of communicating with the manipulator, he begins to doubt everything that he or she thinks or believes to be true.

## 11.	Laying guilt trips on someone

Laying guilt trips on another person is a way of influence that manipulators use to force their victims to do what they want, that is why guilt trips are considered to be one of the favorite and most often used means of subjugation, which the manipulators apply in the relationships with their victims.

With this type of toxic influence, the manipulator at every opportunity accuses the victim either of doing everything wrong, or spoiling everything, or causing the manipulator's failures in something. No matter how hard the victim tries to correct the situation, nothing can help with it - the victim is still to blame, and the manipulator keeps getting angry.

Feeling guilty makes you doubt yourself, even when you catch your significant other on a lie or spot any of his or her manipulative tactics. When the manipulators see how much you feel guilty about the situation, how much you try to fix it, they begin to sympathize with you, and thus they manage to get from you everything they want.

For example, the manipulator tells how much he has problems in his daily life, how difficult it is for him to cope with daily household concerns, how much rent he has to pay monthly, how sad he is about all this. He complains about this to you all the time, so you involuntarily start to feel own involvement in his or her issues, and, out of compassion, you decide to help him or her in something. As a result, over time it will turn out that he has shifted the solution of own issues to you, completely taking off responsibility for them.

Beware of those who do not want to be responsible for their lives, carry their own cross, and solve their problems on their own. As a rule, such people will look for someone who would have done it instead of them. Of course, it does not mean that you should not help people who really need help, no doubt that the feeling of compassion and the desire to help people in a difficult situation is common to all of us, and it's wonderful that we have such a human quality. But there is nothing good in attempts to solve all the problems of the person who does not even want to do something on his or her own to cope with their challenges and is looking for someone, who would do it for him or her. Why? Because in this way it will be easiest for him or her not only to entrust you with responsibility for solving his or her daily issues but also consequently to make you feel guilty every time he or she is dissatisfied with something in the life overall. Thus, one day you will find that you have taken on the main burden of financial, emotional, or psychological consequences associated with your desire to solve all the problematic issues in the life of another person. Surely, you can help another in something when he asks about this, you also can help him or her from time to time, if you can, but you do not have to do this all the time, sacrificing your time, psychological, physical and financial resources to do for another person all the things he or she is able to do himself.

In this case, of course, we do not mean the old people, or those, who suffer some kind of disease, illness or disability and really need help and support of others. Certainly, we should help them if we can.

But if to consider the relationship with average healthy people, who just refuse to manage own life, take responsibility for it, attempt to cope with life challenges himself or herself, you should be aware of possible consequences of your desire to do it instead of them.

In this way, you are exposed to the risk of turning from an altruist into a victim of manipulation of another person.

12.　Playing the victim

So, when you tell someone a sad fact of your life, the experience of life, either troubles or report about feeling bad, you are unlikely to find an attentive, sympathetic and empathic interlocutor in the manipulative individual. Do not reckon on moral support and understanding on his part, since the attention of such personalities, as a rule, is mainly focused on their own personality, their interests, feelings, and experiences. Therefore, in response to your messages about poor health or life situations, you will hear from such a person the stories that they fell much worse, than you do, or experienced situations much more complicated than yours. Also, manipulators often tend to exaggerate, talking about some their bad experience or feeling to make a greater effect, but even if everything they say is true, one thing is important here. In such a situation the purpose of manipulative person is to change the subject, thus moving a focus of the conversation from you to their personality.

No matter how poor is your health, a manipulative person will always try to prove that he or she feels much worse than you. This maneuver is aimed at making you realize that this person needs more attention and compassion, including on your part, but the most basic motive in this tactic is making you always take care about the manipulator more than about yourself, and feel for them, but not for yourself.

When you ask the manipulator to explain such a behavior, they will accuse you of being selfish and eager to be in the spotlight. Thus, the manipulator inclines the victim to think less of him- or herself, and more about the manipulator and his or her needs. Therefore, the victim, being under the influence of such a person, once upon a time may find that he or she devotes his time and compassion to a manipulator, who uses this to his or her advantage.

13.   Using a bait

Using bait, or different kinds of seduction - this is one of the most dangerous tricks that manipulator uses to put his victim on the hook. If we talk about the examples of seduction, as an example it can be a charm, praise, flattery and the support of other people, which manipulator may apply so that to gain your loyalty and trust.

As we said before, before using some of the own tactics, the manipulator will try to understand the character of the person in order to find the approach to the one.

If the manipulator finds that the victim has problems with personal self-esteem and self-image, different psychological complexes, it will be especially easy for him to apply the seduction tactic in relation to the victim. Understanding the nature of their victims enables manipulators to get closer to them, thereon they use the victim's insecurity to become for him or her source of happiness, approval, self-confidence and positive emotions.

14.   Shifting responsibility onto another person

In an unpleasant situation in which the manipulator is guilty, he or she tries to transfer his guilt to the victim, and they do it in such a way so that the victim herself agrees that she is guilty of something. The manipulator will lie in such a way as to prepare the basis for the possibility of lying even more in the future. At the same time, they will complain to everyone around that the object of their manipulation treats him rudely, offensive, and disrespectfully, although all this entirely tend to be untrue. Plus, in addition to slandering their victim, they would say that he or she is crazy and not only do they think so.

The purpose of such pernicious actions is to set control over the victim, undermining her self-confidence and belief in her own perception of reality. The negative influence of such manipulative actions on the psyche is fraught with the fact that the object of manipulation starts doubting own perception, and indeed often takes the blame, regardless of the actual situation. Victims of manipulators, in the end, often feel guilty for what they did not do, and then have to bear responsibility for actions they did not commit, words they did not say, and situations they have nothing to do with. Thus, even if the victims convict the manipulator of lying, they tend to doubt if their assumptions are correct before to question the manipulator's actions.

Manipulative tricks related to seduction tactics ensure that the manipulator will keep the dominating position in their relationships with their victims.

15.   Demonstrating confusion

The manipulator will demonstrate confusion in case of being told some important information, for example, such as the news that their lies are revealed. Under such circumstances, the manipulator will confuse the victim so that he or she would doubt own perception. In time, the victim may find out that he or she believes everything the manipulator tells him or her and trusts the one even more than oneself. This is another way to turn a victim into a "villain".

By virtue of confusion, the manipulator makes the victim believe that all his or her assumptions, statements and actions are erroneous. At the same time, the manipulator offers his own, as he states, "correct" view on the situation, thus inducing the victim to doubt his own rightness and competence, and thereby making the victim believe that he, the manipulator, knows the exact answers to all questions, has the right vision of the situation and makes unmistakable judgments on any occasion. Due to the above techniques, the manipulator not only undermines once again the victim's self-worth, self-esteem, confidence in own perception, but also in this way rises the own importance and competence in the eyes of the victim. The psychological tricks like these enable manipulative individuals easily to set and strengthen their influence and control over another person. To the point, it is also another way for such people to assert themselves at the expense of others.

16.   Intimidation and anger bursts

Using fits of anger to intimidate someone is another psychological technique that manipulators use to get what they want. It is noteworthy that, such anger is not real, but only sham, and is applied by manipulators to frighten or unbalance the victim, in order to increase the one's suggestibility, compliance, and controllability.

In this chapter, we listed and considered in details the tactics most often used by manipulators to make the other person obey and do whatever they want. Based on this information, you can also note that manipulators are good at pretending, playing on weaknesses, but most importantly, they are rarely sincere. Moreover, they will never appreciate your sincerity, but nevertheless, on occasion, they can accuse you of being insensible in case you do not believe in the sincerity of their words, actions, and emotions.

The manipulator can use either of these tactics, or a combination of them, or all of them at once.

The main idea of all these manipulative tactics and tricks is to make you feel that your needs, wants and desires are secondary to their own ones, and no matter what circumstances or facts may be. Plus, these tactics can undermine your self-esteem, which only makes it easier to manipulate you and turn you into the victim of the manipulator.

In this chapter, we will look at the types of manipulators that you might encounter in your daily life. Each of them is distinguished not only by the nature of interaction with others, the manner of behavior but also by the methods of manipulation that they use when communicating with other people.

1. Uninterested manipulators

Manipulators of this type can be characterized as uninterested in anything, indifferent to what is happening around them, including the way how people behave while interacting with them.

When you deal with manipulators of this type, sometimes it seems that it does not matter to them what you do and how you do it, as well as your statements and the emotions you experience. Also, they may seem to be incurious about everything that happens to you, including important moments in your life, festive and sad events.

Acting as if they did not care about anything, these people might attract your attention and arouse in you an interest in his or her person. Despite the fact that you will do everything possible to get to know this person better, he or she will still stay apathetic, but this is only at first glance. They use this kind of behavior aimed at probing your character, getting more information about yourself, inducing you to open up to them.

For manipulators of this type is important to keep you on the hook, without changing their indifferent manner of behavior. Therefore, if you suddenly decide to stop your attempts to "break the ice" in communication with this individual, he or she will try to prevent this, supporting your interest in him or her.

While interaction, these manipulators will not do anything directly to you, but they will use the information got during communicating with you, and playing on your heartstrings they will incline you to do what they want from you.

Initially, they will impel another person to make an emotional contribution to their lives, and then, when the manipulators get to know their victims well enough, they start using their psychological sting to get everything they want from the victims - from the behavioral to the material aspects.

After they have achieved their goal and received from the object of their manipulations whatever they want, they tend to lose any interest in this person and take up the search for a new victim.

2. Unfortunate manipulators

Manipulators of this type are the easiest to identify because their behavior has pronounced features, such as constant complaints about a bad life, poor health, bad luck, etc. These individuals, as a rule, initially try to evoke your sympathy and compassion for them, so that you feel pity for them, but this is not the only thing. In fact, in this case, everything is not as simple as it might seem at first sight.

All people tend to help other people, especially those who are experiencing difficulties, going through life challenges, and this feature is taken into account by manipulators of this type. Unfortunate manipulators appeal to the best essence of the human, and this is one of the ways by which they can penetrate into someone's mind. These individuals use the fact that the victim, guided by a sense of mercy and compassion, will seek to help a person who is in trouble.

People, reacting to someone else's misfortune, do everything in their power to help those who have problems or suffer, but sometimes, while satisfying someone's needs, these responsive people do not realize the fact that they are being manipulated.

Initially, the requests and needs of the manipulator may seem reasonable, but over time they tend to increase and become more complex. Over time, requests quickly turn into requirements, then into orders, and eventually, all claims of the manipulator acquire the character of continuous pumping out your emotional and material resources. Thus, you forget about yourself and other people close to you and do not even realize that all your time and energy is focused on the manipulator. All this can cause the fact that you will sever contacts with many people, and all this ultimately can result into isolation, and this will further impede the opportunities for you and your loved ones to disclose manipulation and pay special attention to this problem.

3. Criticasters

Individuals that belong to this type of manipulators behave more aggressively compared to the two above. Criticasters will actively focus on the behavior of their victims, particularly on their habits and emotional signals; afterward, they will look for sensitive and vulnerable spots in the character of their victims and focus their attention on them. At first, the critics will use their psychological bites implicitly, but over time they become bold more and more in their nagging and negative statements addressed to you.

For manipulators of this type, criticism is a means to get what they want from another person, who, being criticized, will often try to please the kicker, meet his or her expectations, even though the criticaster is setting a high bar for his claims. Nevertheless, the high demands put by the manipulator often turn out to be unattainable for the victim. The constant criticism makes the victim feeling that it does not meet the standards of the manipulator and most likely never be able to satisfy the high level of the expectations of this person. Thus, criticism makes a person feel less valuable, even useless, less competent and much worse than others. And at the same time, diminishing self-esteem and undermining self-confidence of the victim triggers off her or his feeling that the abuser is better, more intelligent, more competent, than the victim is and in general, in many ways surpasses him or her.

Thus, in order to increase self-esteem, the victim will imitate the manipulator in his actions, statements, judgments, and even preferences, so that his or her behavior as a whole will increasingly become like the manipulator's behavior. Or, if the victim retains own individuality, the influence of the manipulator will still affect how she behaves. In other words, the victim will try to guess what the manipulator expects of him or her, and what way he wants the victim to act. When making decisions, statements, actions, the criterion of choice will be not the person's own opinion, but the opinion and evaluation of the manipulator. That is the way how a person gradually loses the feeling of self. The desire to bear a resemblance to another person, who, besides, oppresses you, or your constant attempt to meet someone's expectations, causes a complete erosion and destruction of an identity of the person who plays the role of a victim of manipulation.

4. Bullies

Along with the damage that all these types of manipulators can cause, there is another category of manipulators, and they can be much more dangerous than those we described above.

Although manipulators of this type are reminiscent of criticasters, their danger lies in the fact that they can use intimidation, threats and even violence in order to take another person under their control and force him or her to obey them. This is the most horrible type of manipulators you can come across: they are more aggressive than the kickers and prefer to use the method of a stick, rather than a carrot one, to achieve the desired.

In an effort to get another person to do what they desire, these manipulators often resort to anger, usually with the threat of punishment. Intimidating manipulators do everything to make the victim feel fear because that's how they can most easily get what they want from the one. Relationships with such people become offensive and devoid of respect and dignified treatment.

To deprive the victim of any ability to defend himself psychologically or physically, these manipulators go to great lengths, applying not only threats but also emotional and physical violence.

If we analyze how we are inclined to behave when frightened, or afraid of someone, we in most cases give in to someone much faster than in a situation where we are calm, protected, or occupy a dominant position.

Hardly anyone dares to resist a man who causes us to dread, that directly correlates with feeling afraid that he can hurt us physically.

This is precisely the moment when the bully establishes complete control and domination over the victim.

Now we have a better understanding of what manipulators are, tactics they use and the types that we may encounter in our daily life. So, it is just time to determine the methods of protection from manipulation and manipulators we should keep in mind so that not become one of the victims of emotional and psychological manipulators.

Here we offer the simplest and at the same time effective methods of self-defense from manipulations and their initiators, after mastering which you will be able to protect yourself from toxic relationships, related to emotional and psychological manipulations.

1. In view of the fact that the manipulator is often inclined to work on your emotions to get you out of balance, and thus achieve the desired, try not to take to heart his words and actions. Ability to abstract helps to protect your nerves and keep your balance.

2. Analyze the situation. When the manipulator requires you to do something immediately, not giving time for reflection, take your time, first understand the situation as it comes. Before making any decisions that relate to your relationship with the manipulator or the situations in which both of you take part, analyze the circumstances, weigh the pros

and cons, to count the steps in advance and try to anticipate the possible consequences of your decisions.

3. Do not show your weaknesses. Do not trust a person you do not know very well. But even if you find that you are manipulated by a person close to you, friend or partner, try not to show them your vulnerabilities. It is worth considering that knowing of your weaknesses often becomes a weapon in the hands of other people, which they can use against you. Therefore it is very important to maintain a sufficient level of self-confidence, and not confide to the people who can hurt you.

4. Keep the distance. When you understand that someone is manipulating you, if possible, distance yourself from that person to neutralize the one's negative influence on you and your psychological well-being.

5. Do not try to solve for a person all of his or her problems. If you want to help someone who really needs help, if possible, do it. But do not try to solve all the problems of a person who can do it himself, but does not want to. If you do not want someone to blame you for all the troubles, do not try to be a hero, taking responsibility for solving other people's issues. Do not try to solve

for a person those tasks the one must solve himself.

6. You do not have to feel guilty for something you did not do. If you are sorry for the manipulator, and you want to support him, this does not mean that you have to take the blame for the actions he committed. If he seeks to blame you for what he is guilty of, you should not tolerate it. Be honest with yourself and with other people, and do not agree with a lie about what you really did not do. Every person should be responsible for own actions.

7. If it's about informal relationships, it's important to be able to say "no" when someone is trying to make you do things that you do not want to do. Even if there is a possibility that the manipulator will accuse you of callousness and selfishness, do not give in to this provocation. Be able to politely, but clearly refuse a request, which you can not or do not want to fulfill.

8. Keep your self-esteem and own boundaries. Be able to maintain your self-esteem in any situation; do not let the manipulator undermine it. Keep your identity and respect yourself. Do not pay attention to someone's judgments about what is right for you and what is not. Hear yourself. Do not pay attention to criticism, because the purpose of the

manipulator is to force you to give up on your identity and impose his vision of who you should be and how you must behave. Do not betray yourself, follow your way and own rules. Do not let other people control your life and deprive you of the desire to move forward. Remember that no one has the right to intrude into your life and determine how you should live, except you. You are the master of own destiny.

9. Take notes. Every time when manipulation takes place, or you notice a lie, or you promise something to the manipulator or refused to fulfill his request, write it down for yourself. Notes are worth of doing so that he could not blame you for having a bad memory, and not remembering what you ever said or did. Also, the notes should be taken so that the manipulator could not demand you to do something, on the grounds that you promised to do it once, although really you did not.

10. Take care of yourself. After all, the manipulator often expects you to sacrifice your time, your needs, emotional and physical forces, your financial resources for the sake of them. Emotional manipulation works quite effectively on people who do not care about their main physical or emotional needs. If you feel depressed, you are more likely to be

susceptible to manipulation. Understand that if you do not take care of yourself, no one will do it for you. Moreover, you can not help others if you can not take care of yourself first.

11.	Learn to identify a lie, check the information that the manipulator tells you. Once having caught them in a lie, ask them to explain why they do it but do not provoke a conflict. If the manipulator says that he is lying, because he is afraid of you to be wounded, or is afraid of reproaches from your side, he does not want to quarrel with you, etc., ask them not to lie to you anymore and speak only the truth, whatever it is. If he continues to lie to you anyway, think about whether you need relationships that are built on lies, mistrust, and information concealment. If you can not break the relationship with this person, since this is your relative, close person or colleague, you do not need every time you notice a lie, to argue with a liar and provoke a conflict. Just watch what a person says, how, why, in what situations and for what purpose, and draw conclusions about how to proceed further, so as not to suffer and keep your emotional, psychological balance, and also to protect yourself from pumping out financial funds for inflated, unreasonable and often questionable needs and demands of the manipulator.

12. Finally, you should never agree with the role of the victim, which is imposed on you by another person. The rights of one person do not have more weight than the rights of another person, only on the grounds that another person has more courage or physical strength than another, or has superiority over another person in something else. You do not have to be a means for someone to achieve his goals, and sacrifice your health, physical, emotional and financial well-being to the interests of another person, only on the basis that the one has identified himself as more important, and more worthy, smarter and more talented, than you. Do not expose yourself to a humiliating position, just because someone decided to dominate you. Do not give yourself the offense. You do not have to obey someone against your will, for fear of physical or psychological violence. Do not be afraid. If you are being blackmailed, forced to do something against your desire, being threatened with physical violence, do not be a silent victim, and contact the police for help. After all, impunity gives to the abuser, even more, freedom of action, so your silence will untie his hands even more. If you have been suffering from this problem

for a long time, ask for help from a psychologist, or join psychological support groups for people with the same problem as yours, or just talk to a loved one or close person whom you can trust and rely on. Do not stay alone with your problem

So, we learned what psychological and emotional manipulation is, and how people use it in daily life and in personal relationships to achieve their goals. We examined in detail how some people gradually turn into victims of manipulations and cleared out why this happens.

We also described the most typical psychological tricks that manipulators use to force other people to do what they want and receive get from others certain emotional and material resources. At the same time, we have disclosed the ways how one can identify those manipulative psychological tricks and not get caught on their hook.

Among other things, we considered the types of manipulators we can face with, and examined in detail their character, behavioral style, and the ways they interact with others and with their victims in particular. Also, we figured out how to counteract such individuals and their manipulative influence and protect ourselves from probable psychological harm and losses in the material and financial aspects.

In addition, we suggested the original and simple ways of how to deal with the manipulator and manipulations, if you have already been or are currently being in relationships with them or have to deal with them in business or any other area of life.

Now that you know all this, you are able to be more confident in different situations in which someone tries to manipulate you. To the point, you know how and why people suffer from psychological manipulations under different circumstances, and able to understand the possible causes of the negative feelings you might have during communication with others. Furthermore, you are aware of how to prevent manipulative relationships in the future. But the most important thing is that having read the book, you have acquired the ability to better understand yourself, as well as human nature in general.

Thank
you

9 781983 667817